INTRODUCTION

This paper lays out the Administration's plan to reform America's housing finance market to better serve families and function more safely in a world that has changed dramatically since its original pillars were put in place nearly eighty years ago.

Our plan champions the belief that Americans should have choices in housing that make sense for them and for their families. This means rental options near good schools and good jobs. It means access to credit for those Americans who want to own their own home, which has helped millions of middle class families build wealth and achieve the American Dream. And it means a helping hand for lower-income Americans, who are burdened by the strain of high housing costs.

But our plan also dramatically transforms the role of government in the housing market. In the past, the government's financial and tax policies encouraged housing purchases and real estate investment over other sectors of our economy, and ultimately left taxpayers responsible for much of the risk incurred by a poorly supervised housing finance market.

Going forward, the government's primary role should be limited to robust oversight and consumer protection, targeted assistance for low- and moderate-income homeowners and renters, and carefully designed support for market stability and crisis response. Our plan helps ensure that our nation's economic health will not be jeopardized again by the fundamental flaws in the housing market that existed before the financial crisis. At the same time, this plan recognizes the fragile state of our housing market and is designed to ensure that reforms are implemented at a stable and measured pace to support economic recovery over the next several years.

Under our plan, private markets – subject to strong oversight and standards for consumer and investor protection – will be the primary source of mortgage credit and bear the burden for losses. Banks and other financial institutions will be required to hold more capital to withstand future recessions or significant declines in home prices, and adhere to more conservative underwriting standards that require homeowners to hold more equity in their homes. Securitization, alongside credit from the banking system, should continue to play a major role in housing finance subject to greater risk retention, disclosure, and other key reforms. Our plan is also designed to eliminate unfair capital, oversight, and accounting advantages and promote a level playing field for all participants in the housing market.

The Administration will work with the Federal Housing Finance Agency ("FHFA") to develop a plan to responsibly reduce the role of the Federal National Mortgage Association ("Fannie Mae") and the Federal Home Loan Mortgage Corporation ("Freddie Mac") in the mortgage market and, ultimately, wind down both institutions. We recommend FHFA employ a number of policy levers – including increased guarantee fee pricing, increased down payment requirements, and other measures – to bring private capital back into the mortgage market and reduce taxpayer risk. As the market improves and Fannie Mae and Freddie Mac are wound down, it should be clear that the government is committed to ensuring that Fannie Mae and Freddie Mac have sufficient capital to perform under any guarantees issued now or in the future and the ability to meet any of their debt obligations. We believe that under our current Preferred Stock Purchase Agreements (PSPAs), there is sufficient funding to ensure the orderly and deliberate wind down of Fannie Mae and Freddie Mac, as described in our plan.

Successful reform will require more than just winding down Fannie Mae and Freddie Mac and reducing other government support to the housing market. In addition to fully implementing the reforms in the Dodd-Frank Wall Street Reform and Consumer Protection Act ("Dodd-Frank Act") (Pub. L. 111-203), the Administration will mobilize all tools available to address the nation's broken system of mortgage servicing and foreclosure processing. Taken together, these steps will help restore trust in the underlying foundation of the mortgage market so borrowers, lenders, and investors have the confidence to purchase a home, issue a loan, or make an investment.

The government must also help ensure that all Americans have access to quality housing that they can afford. This does not mean our goal is for all Americans to be homeowners. We should continue to provide targeted and effective support to families with the financial capacity and desire to own a home, but who are underserved by the private market, as well as a range of options for Americans who rent their homes.

Finally, our plan presents several proposals for structuring the government's long-term role in a housing finance system in which the private sector is the dominant provider of mortgage credit. We evaluate these proposals according to their effects on four key criteria: access to mortgage credit; incentives for investment in the housing sector; taxpayer protection; and financial and economic stability. We ask Congress to work with us to determine the right balance of priorities for a new, predominantly private housing finance market as soon as possible.

Reform will not come overnight. Some reforms can take place immediately, like improvements to consumer protection and government oversight, while others will be implemented more gradually as the housing market heals.

We welcome the opportunity to work with Congress, independent regulators and agencies, and a wide range of stakeholders and partners to meet the goals laid out in the pages below.

Housing Finance from the Great Depression to the Great Recession

Nearly eighty years ago, in the midst of the Great Depression, the federal government began implementing sweeping reforms to the American financial system. These reforms – deposit insurance, limits on the risks banks can take, better transparency and investor protections in securities markets, a stronger Federal Reserve – helped build a financial system that provided a solid foundation for America's unprecedented prosperity.

Improving how housing was financed was an important part of these broader Depression-era reforms. In the 1930s, following severe mortgage market disruptions, widespread foreclosures, and sinking homeownership rates, the government created the Federal Housing Administration ("FHA"), Fannie Mae, the Federal Home Loan Banks ("FHLBs") and, several decades later, Freddie Mac to help promote secure and sustainable homeownership for future generations of Americans.

Fannie Mae and Freddie Mac held true to their original mission for many years. They established appropriate benchmarks for conforming loans that drove improved standards within the broader mortgage industry. They helped reduce rates for borrowers by bringing transparency and standardization to the housing finance market. They played a central role in the development of securitization of conventional mortgages, which expanded access to homeownership for responsible borrowers, providing a much-needed link between places with established banking services and growing parts of the country without local funding sources for mortgages. For decades, borrowers, lenders, and investors benefited from the deep, liquid markets these institutions helped establish. This same marketplace gave American families access to simple, straightforward products, protecting them from sudden financial shocks and helping them build savings in their homes.

But in the years leading up to the recent financial crisis, trillions of dollars worth of financial decisions were made across the U.S. economy and around the world on the faulty expectation that national house prices would only rise. Twenty years of economic stability had desensitized every player in the housing market to the possibility that home prices could fall.

Indeed, despite occasional regional price declines, national home values in America had not declined on a consistent basis since the Depression. But in the years leading up to the recent crisis, a robust expansion in credit, fueled by processes and financial instruments designed to shift risk away from originators, combined with other factors, fed a rising demand for housing that lifted prices well above sustainable values. Average home values in many parts of the country skyrocketed. Mortgages became tools for speculative, short-term investments and a means to access easy cash. Lulled into a false sense of an ever-rising real estate market, some homebuyers took on more debt than they could afford to purchase homes beyond their means, and existing homeowners used their homes like ATM machines by converting home equity to cash.

By mid-2006, however, housing prices across a broad range of markets began to turn, eventually declining consistently for the first time since the 1930s. Almost no one in the housing finance market was prepared. Homeowners, investors, and financial institutions – including Fannie Mae and Freddie Mac – did not have enough capital supporting their investments to absorb the resulting losses. In 2008, credit markets froze. Our nation's financial system – which had outgrown and outmaneuvered a regulatory framework largely designed in the 1930s – was driven to the brink of collapse. Millions of Americans lost their jobs, families lost their homes, and small businesses shut down. Fannie Mae and Freddie Mac experienced catastrophic losses and were placed into conservatorship, where they remain today.

Fundamental Flaws in the Housing Finance Market

No single cause can fully explain the crisis. Misbehavior, misjudgments, and missed opportunities – on Wall Street, on Main Street, and in Washington – all came together to push the economy to the brink of collapse. Several fundamental flaws in our housing finance system contributed to the crisis and must be corrected to protect American families from the instabilities and excesses that helped bring us to a crisis point.

- *Poor consumer protections allowed risky, low-quality mortgage products and predatory lending to proliferate:* Unregulated brokers and originators promoted complex mortgage products that "reset" to sharply higher rates after a few years, or required no income documentation or down payment. Some allowed borrowers to defer principal and interest payments, increasing their indebtedness over time. Often, brokers and originators had incentives to steer borrowers into these higher-cost loans, even if they qualified for more affordable options. Some speculators knowingly took on loans they could not afford, betting that future housing price increases would bail them out. Millions of borrowers who purchased these products proved unable to make required payments, resulting in widespread defaults and foreclosures once housing prices started to fall.

- *An inadequate and outdated regulatory regime failed to keep the system in check:* Regulatory boundaries largely unchanged from the 1930s allowed large parts of the financial system that were deeply involved in housing finance to operate with virtually no oversight. To be sure, there were some problems that arose from violations of the law. In many cases, however, weak and fragmented regulation and enforcement also allowed lenders to "shop" for weaker oversight and drove deteriorating standards in lending practices. Securitizers and investors could essentially opt-out of the parts of the system with heavier regulation and use whatever underwriting practices they saw fit. Other actors in the system were allowed to avoid consistent regulation and choose favorable jurisdictions.

- *A complex securitization chain lacked transparency, standardization, and accountability:* The market increasingly relied on an opaque and complex securitization chain – comprised of mortgage brokers, originators, securitizers, ratings agencies, and investors – to provide the money that helped fuel the rapid rise in home prices. Brokers and originators could profit from selling poorly underwritten mortgages to securitizers without regard to those loans' future performance. Ratings agencies and investors failed to recognize that the deterioration in underwriting standards had undermined the quality of complex mortgage-backed securities. An overall lack of transparency and clear rules made it difficult for regulators and investors to track and recognize risk as it moved through the securitization chain.

- *Inadequate capital in the system left financial institutions unprepared to absorb losses.* Systemically-significant financial institutions were not required to hold adequate capital against the true mortgage risk on their balance sheets because these institutions were allowed to hold less capital against securities backed by mortgages than if they kept the same mortgages themselves. When home prices started to fall and these institutions experienced substantial losses, they had inadequate capital to weather the storm, putting the health of the entire financial system and broader economy at risk.

- *The servicing industry was ill-equipped to serve the needs of borrowers, lenders, and investors once housing prices fell.* The servicing industry, which processes borrower payments and forwards the proceeds to investors who own the pool of mortgages, was unprepared and poorly structured to address the higher levels of default and foreclosure that occurred after the housing market collapse. Servicing contracts did a poor job defining the obligations of servicers to minimize losses on defaulting loans. Servicers' flat fee compensation structure also failed to provide appropriate incentives for servicers to invest the time, effort, and resources necessary to prevent foreclosure, even when doing so would have been in both the homeowner and mortgage investors' interests.

The Failure of Fannie Mae and Freddie Mac

Initially, Fannie Mae and Freddie Mac were largely on the sidelines while private markets generated increasingly risky mortgages. Between 2001 and 2005, private-label securitizations of Alt-A and subprime mortgages grew fivefold, yet Fannie Mae and Freddie Mac continued to primarily guarantee fully documented, high-quality mortgages.

But as their combined market share declined – from nearly 70 percent of new originations in 2003 to 40 percent in 2006 – Fannie Mae and Freddie Mac pursued riskier business to raise their market share and increase profits. Not only did they expand their guarantees to new and riskier products, but they also increased their holdings of some of these riskier mortgages on their own balance sheets.

Fannie Mae and Freddie Mac strayed farthest from their core business in 2006 and 2007 – the very moment the housing market was extending credit to the riskiest borrowers and home prices were peaking. When home prices began to fall and adjustable-rate mortgages with low teaser rates reset to higher rates, the Alt-A mortgages that Fannie Mae and Freddie Mac had accumulated started to default at alarming rates.

By 2008, mortgages across the product spectrum, including high-credit, well-documented prime mortgages, were defaulting at historically high rates. Fannie Mae and Freddie Mac's losses had become far too substantial for their thin capital buffers to absorb, and it became clear they would be unable to fully honor their debts and guarantees. In September of 2008, in consultation with the Bush Administration, FHFA placed Fannie Mae and Freddie Mac in conservatorship under the authority provided by the Housing and Economic Recovery Act of 2008 ("HERA") (Pub. L. 110-289), which Congress had passed to support the housing market two months earlier. The Treasury Department agreed to exercise its authority under HERA to provide financial support – to date, over $130 billion – so both Fannie Mae and Freddie Mac could honor their debt and guarantees. These measures, though unfortunate, were necessary to prevent a more severe disruption in the mortgage market and broader economy.

Fannie Mae and Freddie Mac's structural design flaws, combined with failures in management, were the primary cause of their collapse. Although some have suggested affordability goals played a major role, the mistakes that led to the failure of Fannie Mae and Freddie Mac – poor underwriting standards, under pricing risk, and insufficient capital with inadequate regulatory or investor oversight – closely mirrored mistakes in the private-label securities (PLS) market where affordability goals were not a factor. In fact, delinquency rates on many PLS securities and other loans held by banks and other private market institutions were far higher than on the loans held by Fannie Mae and Freddie Mac, including loans qualifying for the affordability goals. While Fannie Mae and Freddie Mac's affordability goals were poorly designed and did not effectively serve their purposes (as detailed below), fundamental structural flaws and poor decision-making are the principal reasons these institutions failed.

- *Fannie Mae and Freddie Mac's profit-maximizing structure undermined their public mission.* Fannie Mae and Freddie Mac's congressional charters require them to promote market stability and access to mortgage credit. But their private shareholder structure, coupled with a weak oversight regime, encouraged management to take on excessive risk in order to retain market share and maximize profits, jeopardizing their ability to support the mortgage market and leaving taxpayers to bear major losses. Their pursuit of profit leading up to the financial crisis caused them to fail when their broader public mandate to support the market was needed most.

- *Fannie Mae and Freddie Mac's perceived government backing conferred unfair advantages.* Fannie Mae and Freddie Mac benefited from preferential tax treatment, far lower capital requirements, and a widely perceived government guarantee – the commonly held assumption that large losses would be backstopped by the taxpayer. These advantages gave them substantial pricing power that helped them dominate segments of the market in which they participated, build up large investment portfolios at a cost far lower than their competitors, and take on irresponsible risks through their guarantee business that ultimately resulted in their failure.

- *Fannie Mae and Freddie Mac's capital standards were unfair and inadequate.* Fannie Mae and Freddie Mac were required to hold far less capital than other regulated private institutions. Since they did not have to maintain higher levels of capital, they could set the fee that they charged to guarantee mortgage-backed securities at artificially low levels. It also left them with an inadequate cushion to absorb losses once the housing crisis hit.

- *Fannie Mae and Freddie Mac's regulator was structurally weak and ineffective.* The Office of Federal Housing Enterprise Oversight ("OFHEO"), Fannie Mae and Freddie Mac's previous regulator, did not have adequate enforcement mechanisms or authority to set capital standards to constrain risky behavior. Over the years, Fannie Mae and Freddie Mac's aggressive lobbying efforts had successfully defeated efforts to bring them under closer supervision.

The financial crisis also exacerbated fundamental flaws in the FHLBs, which help mostly insured depository institutions access liquidity and capital to compete in an increasingly competitive marketplace. Prior to the crisis, the FHLBs suffered from inadequate regulatory oversight, and were allowed to build large investment portfolios that subjected them to excess risk, while providing concentrated funding to banks engaging in unsound business practices. Today, eight of the twelve banks are under regulatory orders with respect to their capital or have voluntarily suspended dividends or the repurchase of excess stock.

Because each of the twelve FHLBs is also liable for the losses of other FHLBs, additional losses could adversely affect the entire FHLB system, damaging the mortgage finance market and potentially constraining access to capital for financial institutions. Reforms to the FHLB system are necessary to restore its important primary role of providing a stable source of mortgage credit for financial institutions of all sizes.

The Current State of the Housing Market

Since taking office in January 2009, the Obama Administration has acted to help stabilize the housing market and provide critical support for struggling homeowners. The Administration worked with Congress to put in place expanded tax credits for first-time homebuyers, additional support for state and local housing agencies, neighborhood stabilization and community development programs, mortgage modification and refinancing initiatives, housing counseling programs, expanded support for mortgage credit through FHA, and strengthened consumer protections. The Administration has also provided ongoing financial support for Fannie Mae and Freddie Mac through the PSPAs following the Bush Administration's decision to put that support in place and FHFA's decision to place them into conservatorship.

These policies helped avert a deeper economic collapse and a more severe housing crisis. However, the housing market remains fragile and will take years to fully recover. An elevated unemployment rate, lower household wealth, and higher credit standards are constraining demand for housing. Sales of new and existing homes are well below their recent peaks. At the same time, the large inventory of unsold homes, including a backlog of foreclosed homes that have yet to appear on the market, will take an extended period to work through the system. As a result of both supply and demand factors, housing construction is at historically low levels, and home prices remain weak.

TOWARDS A NEW SYSTEM OF HOUSING FINANCE

The Obama Administration has already begun the critical process of reforming our nation's housing finance market. The Dodd-Frank Act, enacted in July 2010, provides vital protections for consumers and investors that will help end abusive practices in the mortgage market and improve the stability of the overall housing finance system.

Since Fannie Mae and Freddie Mac were placed into conservatorship, the FHFA has monitored their business operations closely and strengthened underwriting standards, reducing risk to the American taxpayers. Since 2008, FICO scores and loan-to-value ratios – both key measures of how likely a borrower will be to make mortgage payments – are meaningfully better on new mortgages. Fannie Mae and Freddie Mac have also increased their guarantee fees and adjusted their pricing to better reflect risk. The FHA has also implemented important changes and reforms over the last two years, including strengthening underwriting standards, improving processes and operations, and raising premiums to improve its financial condition.

But these measures are only first steps. We must move forward with additional reforms to better protect taxpayers and improve the long-term health of the housing market.

The Obama Administration's reform plan is designed to:

1. Pave the way for a robust private mortgage market by reducing government support for housing finance and winding down Fannie Mae and Freddie Mac on a responsible timeline.

2. Address fundamental flaws in the mortgage market to protect borrowers, help ensure transparency for investors, and increase the role of private capital.

3. Target the government's vital support for affordable housing in a more effective and transparent manner.

Any responsible reform effort that addresses the flaws in the pre-crisis housing market will make credit less easily available than before the crisis. Any such changes should occur at a measured pace that allows borrowers to adjust to the new market, that preserves widespread access to affordable mortgages for creditworthy borrowers, including lower-income Americans, and that supports, rather than threatens, the nation's economic recovery.

I. Paving the Way for a Robust Private Mortgage Market

In the wake of the financial crisis, private capital has not sufficiently returned to the mortgage market, leaving Fannie Mae, Freddie Mac, FHA, and the Government National Mortgage Association ("Ginnie Mae") to insure or guarantee more than nine out of every ten new mortgages.

Under normal market conditions, the essential components of housing finance – buying houses, lending money, determining how best to invest capital, and bearing credit risk – are fundamentally private sector activities. Although the government still has an important role to play in housing finance, private markets – subject to strong oversight and standards for consumer and investor protection – should be the primary source of mortgage credit and bear the burden for losses. The Obama Administration, in consultation with FHFA and Congress, will work to restrict the areas of mortgage finance in which Fannie Mae, Freddie Mac, and the FHLBs operate, so that overall government support is substantially reduced.

Our commitment to ensuring Fannie Mae and Freddie Mac have sufficient capital to honor any guarantees issued now or in the future and meet any of their debt obligations remains unchanged. Ensuring these institutions have the financial capacity to meet their obligations is essential to continued stability, and the Administration will not waver from its commitment. Given Fannie Mae and Freddie Mac's current role in the mortgage market, we must proceed carefully with reform to ensure government support is withdrawn at a pace that does not undermine economic recovery. We believe that under the PSPAs, there is sufficient funding to ensure the orderly and deliberate wind down of Fannie Mae and Freddie Mac, as described in our plan.

Winding Down Fannie Mae and Freddie Mac on a responsible timeline

The Administration will work with FHFA to determine the best way to responsibly reduce Fannie Mae and Freddie Mac's role in the market and ultimately wind down both institutions, creating the conditions for private capital to play the predominant role in housing finance. These efforts must be undertaken at a deliberate pace, which takes into account the impact that these changes will have on borrowers and the housing market.

- *Increasing guarantee fees to bring in more private capital.* We support ending the unfair capital advantages that Fannie Mae and Freddie Mac previously enjoyed and recommend FHFA require that they price their guarantees as if they were held to the same capital

12

standards as private banks or financial institutions. This will mean that the price of the guarantee offered by Fannie Mae and Freddie Mac explicitly reflects its risk, and will help the private market compete on a level playing field, reducing Fannie Mae and Freddie Mac's market share over time. Although the pace of these price changes will depend significantly on market conditions, such changes should be phased in over the next several years.

- *Increasing private capital ahead of Fannie Mae and Freddie Mac guarantees.* In addition to increasing guarantee pricing, we will encourage Fannie Mae and Freddie Mac to pursue additional credit-loss protection from private insurers and other capital providers. We also support increasing the level of private capital ahead of Fannie Mae and Freddie Mac's guarantees by requiring larger down payments by borrowers. Going forward, we support gradually increasing the level of required down payment so that any mortgages insured by Fannie Mae or Freddie Mac eventually have at least a ten percent down payment.

- *Reducing conforming loan limits.* The conforming loan limit is the maximum size of a loan that Fannie Mae and Freddie Mac are allowed to guarantee. In order to further scale back the enterprises' share of the mortgage market, the Administration recommends that Congress allow the temporary increase in limits that was approved in 2008 to expire as scheduled on October 1, 2011 and revert to the limits established under HERA. We will work with Congress to determine appropriate conforming loan limits in the future, taking into account cost-of-living differences across the country. As a result of these reforms, larger loans for more expensive homes will once again be funded only through the private market.

- *Winding down Fannie Mae and Freddie Mac's investment portfolio.* Fannie Mae and Freddie Mac were allowed to behave like government-backed hedge funds, managing large investment portfolios for the profit of their shareholders with the risk ultimately falling largely on taxpayers. The PSPAs require a reduction in this risk-taking by winding down their investment portfolios at an annual pace of no less than 10 percent.

Implementing a wind down of Fannie Mae and Freddie Mac's future participation in the housing market requires recognition of both the fragile state of that market today and the private sector's need for clarity about the speed with which that transition will take place. As the market begins to heal and private investors return, we will seek opportunities, wherever possible, to accelerate Fannie Mae and Freddie Mac's withdrawal.

Returning FHA to its traditional role as targeted lender of affordable mortgages

In addition to winding down Fannie Mae and Freddie Mac, FHA should return to its pre-crisis role as a targeted provider of mortgage credit access for low- and moderate-income Americans and first-time homebuyers. (Today, FHA's market share is nearly 30 percent, compared to its historic role of between 10-15 percent.) As Fannie Mae and Freddie Mac's presence in the market shrinks, the Administration will coordinate program changes at FHA to ensure that the private market – not FHA – picks up that new market share.

To accomplish this objective, we recommend decreasing the maximum loan size that can qualify for FHA insurance – first by allowing the present increase in those limits to expire as scheduled on October 1, 2011, and then by reviewing whether those limits should be further decreased moving forward. As we begin to pursue increased pricing for guarantees at Fannie Mae and Freddie Mac, we will also increase the price of FHA mortgage insurance. We have already acted on this front, raising premiums two times since the beginning of this Administration. And we will put in place another 25 basis point increase in the annual mortgage insurance premium that is detailed in the President's 2012 Budget. This will continue the ongoing effort to strengthen the capital reserve account of FHA, and put it in a better position to gradually shrink its market share. Going forward we will coordinate reforms of Fannie Mae and Freddie Mac with changes at FHA to help ensure the private market, not FHA, fills the market opportunities created by reform.

Ensuring FHLB support for small- and medium-sized financial institutions

The Administration believes the FHLBs have played a vital role in our housing finance system by helping smaller financial institutions effectively access liquidity to compete in an increasingly competitive marketplace. But these institutions also developed significant weaknesses as the housing market evolved that should be addressed as part of housing finance reform. HERA has already placed the FHLBs under stricter regulatory oversight, but further reform is required. We will also work with Congress to consider additional means of advance funding for mortgage credit, including potentially the development of a covered bond market.

- *Focusing on small- and medium-sized financial institutions.* The Administration supports allowing each financial institution to be an active member in only a single FHLB Bank. We also support limiting the level of advances, which would only have an impact on large financial institutions that can access capital markets already.

- *Reducing portfolio investments.* Similar to Fannie Mae and Freddie Mac, several of the FHLBs were allowed to build up large investment portfolios. These portfolios should be reduced and their composition altered to better serve the FHLB's mission of providing liquidity and access to capital for insured depository institutions. We support FHFA's efforts to address this issue, and we will work with Congress to provide clarity to the FHLB's investment authority.

Improving coordination among existing government housing finance programs

In addition to changing the level of government support for the housing market, we also must reform the way government support is delivered. The Department of Housing and Urban Development, the Department of Agriculture, and the Department of Veterans Affairs will set up a task force to explore ways in which their housing finance programs can be better coordinated, or even consolidated, to serve the public more effectively. Though they serve different targeted groups of Americans, their programs and borrowers will benefit from greater coordination of systems, information, and market standards.

II. Restoring Trust and Integrity in the Broader Housing Market

Addressing Fannie Mae, Freddie Mac, FHA, and the FHLBs alone will not give rise to a housing finance market that meets the needs of families, lenders, and investors. Nor will it guarantee that private markets can effectively play a more dominant role in the mortgage market. Fundamental flaws occurred at almost every link in the housing finance chain.

The Administration supports the vigorous implementation of reforms to help address pre-crisis flaws and rebuild trust and integrity in the mortgage market. Taken together, these reforms will improve consumer protection, support the creation of safe, high-quality mortgage products with strong underwriting standards, restore the integrity of the securitization market, restructure the servicing industry, and establish clear and consolidated regulatory oversight.

The Dodd-Frank Act laid the groundwork for many of these reforms. We will implement its provisions in a thoughtful manner to protect borrowers and promote stability across the housing finance markets. Together, these reforms will form the foundation of a market in which borrowers, lenders, investors – along with the broader economy – will all be better off.

Empowering consumers to avoid unfair practices and make fully informed decisions

The Administration is committed to full implementation of the Dodd-Frank Act's consumer protection provisions, including the following:

- *Curbing abusive practices.* Under rules to be developed by the Bureau of Consumer Financial Protection ("CFPB"), which was created by the Dodd-Frank Act, lenders will be prohibited from originating high-cost loans with certain abusive features, and mortgage brokers and other originators will be prohibited from accepting financial rewards for steering borrowers into more expensive products than those for which they are qualified.

- *Promoting choice and clarity.* The CFPB also will have the authority to set clear, consistent rules that allow financial services providers to compete on a level playing field and let consumers clearly see the costs and features of consumer financial products and services. The CFPB will take steps to improve and simplify the required disclosures for mortgage loan transactions to promote fairness, transparency, and competition in the mortgage market.

- *Stronger underwriting standards, including requiring lenders to verify ability to pay.* Under rules to be prescribed by the CFPB, lenders will be required to make a reasonable and good-faith determination that all borrowers have a reasonable ability to repay their mortgage, including by verifying a borrower's income.

Increasing transparency, standardization, and accountability in the securitization chain

The Administration believes the securitization market should continue to play a key role in housing finance. That market, however, requires meaningful reform so private investors can confidently participate in the housing market and provide an alternative funding source for mortgages outside of the traditional banking system and government-supported institutions.

- *Requiring originators and securitizers to retain risk.* The Administration is working with federal regulators to set rules requiring securitizers or originators to retain five percent of a security's credit risk when sold to investors. Combined with an exemption for mortgages that meet high underwriting standards (Qualified Residential Mortgages, or "QRM"), this requirement will improve alignment of interests between mortgage originators, securitizers, and investors. Rules will be finalized in 2011 and become effective in 2012.

- *Improving access to information among all market participants.* The SEC will implement Dodd-Frank Act provisions that set stricter disclosure and reporting requirements so that regulators and investors can more easily understand the underlying collateral and risks of securities.

- *Strengthen transparency and disclosure in credit ratings agencies' analysis.* The Securities and Exchange Commission ("SEC") will establish an Office of Credit Ratings. This new office will have dedicated compliance resources with the ability to improve disclosure for ratings methodologies, set new requirements to prohibit conflicts of interest, and authorize the SEC to deregister ratings agencies that perform poorly.

Increasing capital standards to improve the safety and stability of the financial system

The Basel III Capital Accords will substantially increase the overall amount of capital that banks are required to hold on their balance sheets. These measures will improve the ability of banks to withstand future downturns, declines in home prices, and other sudden economic shocks, which will help improve the safety and stability of the financial system and broader economy. These new standards will also require banks to hold larger capital buffers against higher-risk mortgages that have a greater risk of default, providing strong incentives to originate higher-quality mortgages.

Strengthening regulatory oversight

The Dodd-Frank Act provides a comprehensive approach to monitor and constrain excessive risk in the financial system, and to strengthen the transparency and resilience of financial markets.

- *Closing regulatory gaps.* The newly created Financial Stability Oversight Council ("FSOC") has the authority to require consolidated supervision of any financial firm – regardless of legal form – whose failure could pose a threat to financial stability. The Act also eliminates regulatory arbitrage for nationally chartered depository institutions by eliminating the Office of Thrift Supervision and moving that authority into the Office of the Comptroller of the Currency.

- *Monitoring systemic risk.* The Dodd-Frank Act creates accountability in the FSOC for taking a comprehensive approach to monitoring the nation's financial system. The FSOC is charged with identifying threats to the financial stability of the United States, promoting market discipline, and responding to emerging risks to the stability of the United States financial system, including mortgage markets.

Improving mortgage servicing and foreclosure processing

The Administration supports several immediate and near-term reforms to correct problems in mortgage servicing and foreclosure processing and help prevent their recurrence.

- *Establishing national standards for mortgage servicing.* Servicers should manage each loan that they service promptly and appropriately. The Administration supports national servicing standards that better align incentives and provide clarity and consistency to borrowers and investors regarding their treatment by servicers, especially in the event of delinquency.

- *Reforming servicing compensation to align industry incentives.* The Administration is working with FHFA, in coordination with HUD, to explore alternative servicing compensation structures to align industry incentives. Currently, servicers collect a flat fee that does not adjust to reflect the amount of work they are required to perform, resulting in overpayment for servicing current loans and underpayment for servicing delinquent loans. A compensation structure that corrects for the current structure's shortcomings could help ensure servicers are appropriately incentivized to invest the time and effort to work with troubled borrowers to avoid default or foreclosure.

- *Improving treatment of lien priority.* We should reduce conflicts of interests between holders of first and second mortgages and improve transparency for lenders and borrowers regarding the total debt secured by a given piece of property. Mortgage documents should require disclosure of second liens. In addition, mortgage documents should define the process for modifying a second lien in the event that the first lien becomes delinquent. This will prevent a second lien from standing in the way of a first lien modification and help prevent avoidable foreclosures. Finally, we should consider options for allowing primary mortgage holders to restrict, in certain circumstances, additional debt secured by the same property.

III. A System with Transparent and Targeted Support for Access and Affordability

The Administration believes that we must continue to take the necessary steps to ensure that Americans have access to an adequate range of affordable housing options. This does not mean all Americans should become homeowners. Instead, we should make sure that all Americans who have the credit history, financial capacity, and desire to own a home have the opportunity to take that step. At the same time, we should ensure that there are a range of affordable options for the 100 million Americans who rent, whether they do so by choice or necessity.

In the past, broader government efforts to support affordability through Fannie Mae and Freddie Mac's affordable housing goals proved inefficient and ineffective. Their affordability goals were inadequately responsive to the unique needs of underserved families and communities. They were misaligned with lending in the primary market. And most egregiously, they did not exclude high-cost, predatory loans. As we establish new ways to ensure access and affordability, we must learn from these failed efforts and design policies that are better targeted, more transparent, and focused on providing support that is financially sustainable for families and communities.

We recommend focusing initially on four primary areas of reform:

- A reformed and strengthened FHA.

- A commitment to affordable rental housing.

- Measures to ensure that capital is available to creditworthy borrowers in *all* communities, including rural areas, economically distressed regions, and low-income communities.

- A flexible and transparent funding source to support targeted access and affordability initiatives.

A reformed and strengthened FHA

The Administration is committed to ensuring creditworthy first-time homebuyers and families with modest incomes can access a mortgage. The Administration will make sure that creditworthy borrowers that have incomes up to the median level for their area have access to these mortgages, but we will do so in a way that does not allow FHA to expand during normal economic times to a share of the market that is unhealthy or unsustainable.

To make sure that FHA is financially strong enough to provide this key support, and that those taking out FHA-insured single-family loans are taking on sustainable mortgages, the Administration will explore ways to further reduce the risk exposure of FHA. While FHA has already changed its policy to require that borrowers with lower FICO scores put down larger down payments, FHA will consider other options, such as lowering the maximum loan-to-value ratio for qualifying mortgages more broadly. In considering how to apply such options, FHA will continue to balance the need to manage prudently the risk to FHA and the borrower with its efforts to ensure access to affordable loans for lower- and middle-income Americans.

We will work with Congress to give FHA more flexibility to respond to stress in the housing market and manage its risk more effectively. This will mean giving FHA flexibility to adjust fees and programmatic parameters more nimbly than it can today. FHA should also have the technology and talent needed to run what should be a world-class financial institution.

A renewed commitment to affordable rental housing

As we move forward to address the challenges of affordability and access, we must address how those issues impact renters. Today, renters often face significant affordability challenges. Half of all renters spend more than a third of their income on housing, and a quarter spend more than half. And for low-income renters, adequate and affordable homes are increasingly scarce. For every 100 extremely low-income American families, for example, only 32 adequate rental homes are affordable.

Promoting a housing finance market that provides liquidity and capital to support affordable rental options can alleviate the high rental burdens that many low-income households face. It can also expand rental options for low-income households in urban, suburban, and rural communities of opportunity, with good jobs for parents and quality schools for children.

Private credit markets have generally underserved multifamily rental properties that offer affordable rents, preferring to invest in high-end developments. By contrast, Fannie Mae and Freddie Mac developed expertise in profitably providing financing to the middle of the rental market, where housing is generally affordable to moderate-income families. As we wind down Fannie Mae and Freddie Mac, it will be critical to find ways to maintain funding to this segment of the market.

The Administration will explore ways to provide greater support for rental housing. One option would be to do so by expanding FHA's capacity to support lending to the multifamily market. Key to this would be utilizing existing multifamily expertise so that FHA and other entities continue the industry's current best practices and retain valuable human capital. We will consider a range of reforms, such as risk-sharing with private lenders, to reduce the risk to FHA and the taxpayer, and the development of programs dedicated to hard-to-reach property segments, including the smaller properties that contain one-third of all rental apartments.

Ensuring that capital is available to creditworthy borrowers in all communities

We will work to ensure that all mortgage market participants are complying with laws that prohibit discrimination in providing capital to borrowers and communities. To support that effort, we will work with Congress to require greater transparency in the mortgage market, requiring securitizers to disclose information on the credit, geographic, and demographic characteristics of the underlying loans they package into securities. This will make it easier to determine whether market participants are complying with their legal obligations, and also make clear to the public what communities these institutions are and are not serving.

We will work with Congress to ensure that *all* communities and families – including those in rural and economically distressed areas, as well as those that are low- and moderate-income – have the access to capital needed for sustainable homeownership and a range of rental options. We will consider measures to make sure that secondary market participants are providing capital to all communities in ways that reflect activity in primary markets, consistent with their obligations of safety and soundness.

Dedicated funds for targeted homeownership and rental affordability

Although FHA and other federal affordable housing policies do a great deal to provide access and affordability, we recognize that a more balanced system will require additional resources to address clear gaps. The Administration will thus advocate for a dedicated, budget-neutral financing mechanism to support homeownership and rental housing objectives that current policies cannot adequately address. This funding stream would support the development and preservation of more affordable rental housing for the lowest-income families to address serious supply shortages, similar to the Housing Trust Fund that the President has proposed to be capitalized. It would support down-payment assistance and counseling to help qualified low- and moderate-income homebuyers, in a form that does not expose them or financial institutions to excessive risk or cost. We would scale up support for proven nonprofit partnerships for affordable housing production and preservation that can attract much larger amounts of private capital. And funding would help to overcome market failures that make it hard to develop a secondary market for targeted affordable housing mortgages, such as that for small rental properties.

These components target specific needs in flexible ways that can engage a range of partners and respond to local priorities and opportunities. We will work with Congress to ensure that funding will be budget neutral, transparent, and targeted to clearly defined objectives and programs.

A RESPONSIBLE PATH FORWARD FOR REFORM

The reform measures outlined in this report will help reshape the housing finance market by putting private capital back at the center of a healthier system, reducing taxpayer risk, and increasing protections for consumers and investors. However, given the still-fragile state of the housing market, implementing these reforms fully will take time. The Administration will proceed deliberately so that the mortgage-finance chain and the broader capital markets are not disrupted during this transition.

The importance of a responsible transition

Proceeding with a prudent transition plan and providing the necessary financial support to Fannie Mae and Freddie Mac during that period is essential to protecting the health of the economic recovery and is in the best interests of taxpayers.

A careful transition path offers the best prospects for maximizing recovery on the investments we have made in these institutions and minimizing future losses. Prematurely constraining Fannie Mae and Freddie Mac's ability to guarantee loans or precipitously winding them down could limit the availability of mortgage credit, shock the housing market, and expose taxpayers to additional losses on the loans Fannie Mae and Freddie Mac already guarantee.

The losses that the federal government has covered at Fannie Mae and Freddie Mac under HERA authority are virtually all attributable to bad loans that those firms took on during the height of the housing bubble. Over the last two years, Fannie Mae and Freddie Mac have implemented stricter underwriting standards and increased their pricing. As a result, the new loans being guaranteed by Fannie Mae and Freddie Mac today are of much higher quality than in the past and are unlikely to pose a significant risk of loss to taxpayers.

As Fannie Mae and Freddie Mac are wound down, we must design a transition that allows for continued support of the housing market, so that Americans continue to have the ability to take out a mortgage to buy a home or refinance their existing mortgage. We will continue to work with FHFA to ensure that talent is retained so that mortgage credit continues to flow and risk is contained during the transition, and that the wind down is as successful as possible and supports taxpayers' interests.

The government is committed to ensuring that Fannie Mae and Freddie Mac have sufficient capital to perform under any guarantees issued now or in the future and the ability to meet any of their debt obligations. The Administration will not pursue policies or reforms in a way that would impair the ability of Fannie Mae and Freddie Mac to honor their obligations.

A path forward

Determining the appropriate path for how to responsibly wind down Fannie Mae and Freddie Mac and reduce the size of FHA will be challenging and will require great care. As members of the Federal Housing Finance Oversight Board ("FHFOB"), the Advisory Board to FHFA, the Secretaries of Treasury and HUD will make recommendations on the appropriate mix of incentives and deadlines for FHFA to pursue to wind down these institutions at a pace that recognizes the fragile state of the housing market.

We support the creation of a joint FHFA and FHA working group to consider changes to pricing and other standards. We recommend that FHFA and FHA seek comment from the public on the most appropriate pace of the transition and issue a timeline for tightening standards and raising pricing. This working group should provide regular updates to the FHFOB and FSOC, as reforms are implemented. Throughout the transition, FHFA and FHA should continue to seek comment and revise timelines as necessary to account for changing market conditions and accelerate the transition where possible.

As the reforms outlined in the Administration's plan are implemented and new standards at Fannie Mae, Freddie Mac, FHA, and the FHLBs are established, we will ultimately need to complete the transition to a more privatized market. We face a consequential choice about how to structure the government's ultimate role within that market. This report outlines three proposals for Congress and the Administration to consider together. Each of these proposals has unique advantages and disadvantages that deserve thorough evaluation through a robust public dialogue.

Options for the Long-Term Structure of Housing Finance

There has been robust discussion about the long-term future of the American mortgage market and a wide range of options proposed for its reform that differ both in the structure and scale of the government's future role.

As part of this discussion, we considered the range of ways other countries support housing finance. Though there are lessons to be drawn from the diversity of systems, they are complex. In most countries lacking a widely available guarantee or other means of direct government support, mortgages are financed through the banking system, which often enjoys indirect government backing. Some countries utilize their regulatory framework, or establish firm underwriting standards, to promote liquid mortgage markets. And some countries, particularly in Europe, use so-called covered bonds to channel credit to housing.

Like the U.S., several countries have government-supported entities that guarantee or hold mortgages, though in none are they as large as they have historically been in the United States. The U.S. is also the only high-income country in which securitization plays a major role in housing finance. In countries where securitization is present, it generally plays a smaller role and takes different forms than those we are familiar with in this country. The U.S. system, however, is one of the only countries in the world where the majority of mortgages are pre-payable, 30-year fixed-rate mortgages.

Although international comparisons offer useful lessons and new ideas, we believe that Americans' housing needs can best be met by a system that takes four key factors into consideration:

Access to Mortgage Credit. Government support for housing finance can expand access to mortgage credit for creditworthy American families. By attracting additional capital into the housing finance system, it can lower the cost of mortgages and increase the availability of certain kinds of mortgage products, such as the 30-year, fixed-rate mortgage. The government can also help standardize the national mortgage market by setting specific criteria for the types of mortgages that it will support. Government support can also increase access to secondary markets for smaller lenders and community banks, promoting a more competitive market and minimizing consolidation.

Incentive for Investment in Housing. Government support makes investment in housing more attractive. While this can broaden access and lower costs for borrowers and communities, it can also draw investment away from other areas that may lead to greater long-term growth or job creation and it can inflate the value of housing assets, possibly leading to larger boom and bust cycles. Without government support, however, some of the capital invested in the housing market today may simply move to investments outside the United States that offer better risk-weighted returns. Other government policies, such as tax incentives like the mortgage interest deduction and other tax credits can also encourage investment towards housing over other sectors in the economy.

Taxpayer Protection. Any time the government stands behind a loan, even indirectly, it takes on some degree of risk. While the government can charge market participants an insurance premium for accepting that risk, pricing risk properly can be difficult. If the government does not charge a fair price, it may encourage excessive risk-taking and increase the likelihood that the taxpayer will be forced to bear the cost of the government's losses. Political pressure to lower the price of government support increases the odds that the government will misprice risk and put taxpayers at risk. Requiring private capital to come ahead of government guarantees or providing a way to ensure taxpayer losses are repaid through future assessments, such as higher fees, may mitigate these risks.

Financial and Economic Stability. Government support can help promote financial stability by ensuring the flow of credit through periods of economic stress. However, if not properly structured, it can also encourage the private market to take on excessive risk and potentially destabilize the system.

While the options that have been proposed vary widely, each can be viewed as posing trade-offs between the four factors mentioned above.

Some advocates and experts have proposed approaches to our housing finance system that starkly illustrate this trade-off: one advocates a near complete privatization of the mortgage market, while others advocate for its near complete nationalization. Under the former, the government would restrict support for the mortgage market to narrowly targeted subsidies for lower-income Americans. Under the latter, the government would provide an explicit guarantee and directly bear most of the credit risk for almost the entire mortgage market.

While each of these approaches has positive attributes, the Administration does not believe that either represents a viable long-term strategy for the nation's housing market. Complete privatization would limit access to, and increase the cost of, mortgages for most Americans too dramatically and leave the government with very little it can do to ensure liquidity during a crisis. Near-complete nationalization runs too high a risk of crowding out private capital, distorting investment decisions, and putting too much taxpayer money at risk.

The Administration believes that the right course falls between these two extremes, with the government's role in the future mortgage market striking a balance between the factors outlined above: creditworthy Americans should have broad access to credit, but not at a cost of excessive taxpayer risk, distorted markets, or financial instability.

With that in mind, we should consider three possible courses for long-term reform.

Option 1: Privatized system of housing finance with the government insurance role limited to FHA, USDA and Department of Veterans' Affairs' assistance for narrowly targeted groups of borrowers

This option would dramatically reduce the government's role in insuring or guaranteeing mortgages, limiting it to FHA and other programs targeted to creditworthy lower- and moderate-income borrowers. While the government would continue to provide access for this targeted segment of borrowers, it would leave the vast majority of the mortgage market to the private sector.

The strength of this option is that it would minimize distortions in capital allocation across sectors, reduce moral hazard in mortgage lending and drastically reduce direct taxpayer exposure to private lenders' losses. With less incentive to invest in housing, more capital will flow into other areas of the economy, potentially leading to more long-run economic growth and reducing the inflationary pressure on housing assets. Risk throughout the system may also be reduced, as private actors will not be as inclined to take on excessive risk without the assurance of a government guarantee behind them. And finally, direct taxpayer risk exposure to private losses in the mortgage market would be limited to the loans guaranteed by FHA and other narrowly-targeted government loan programs: no longer would taxpayers be at direct risk for guarantees covering most of the nation's mortgages.

Though these are indeed significant benefits, this option has particularly acute costs in its potential impact on access to credit for many Americans. While FHA would continue to provide access to mortgage credit for low- and moderate-income Americans, the cost of mortgage credit for those who do not qualify for an FHA-insured loan – the majority of borrowers – would likely increase. While mortgage rates are likely to rise somewhat under any responsible reform proposal, including the three outlined here, the effect could be larger under this option. In particular, it may be more difficult for many Americans to afford the traditional pre-payable, 30-year fixed-rate mortgage. Additionally, smaller lenders and community banks could have a difficult time competing for business outside of the FHA segment of the market, which may in turn impact access to lending in the communities they have traditionally served more effectively than larger institutions.

Another concern with this option is the ability of the government to effectively step in to ensure access to capital during a crisis. Congress, FHA, the Federal Reserve, and other regulators would be able to play the countercyclical role that they have played in the recent downturn, but it is unlikely that they could play a still more robust role as might be needed in the absence of broader government support in the market. And absent sufficient government support to mitigate a credit crisis, there would be greater risk of a more severe downturn, and thus the risk of greater cost to the taxpayer. A related risk would exist if investors believe that the government would inevitably step in to save whatever private financial institutions or banks have become necessary to maintain the flow of mortgage credit. If so, this option will potentially fail to eliminate the risk of moral hazard.

Option 2: Privatized system of housing finance with assistance from FHA, USDA and Department of Veterans' Affairs for narrowly targeted groups of borrowers and a guarantee mechanism to scale up during times of crisis

As in the option above, FHA and other narrowly targeted programs would provide access to mortgage credit for low- and moderate-income borrowers, but the government's overall role in the housing finance system would be dramatically reduced. In this option, however, the government would also develop a backstop mechanism to ensure access to credit during a housing crisis.

This backstop would maintain a minimal presence in the market during normal times, but would be ready to scale up to a larger share of the market as private capital withdraws in times of financial stress. One approach would be to price the guarantee fee at a sufficiently high level that it would only be competitive in the absence of private capital. It would thus only expand when needed, and that need would be dictated by the market. An alternative approach would restrict the amount of public insurance sold to the private market in normal times, but allow the amount of insurance offered to ramp up to stabilize the market in times of stress.

The strength of this proposal is that it would be designed to address one of the primary concerns associated with the prior model – the inability of the government to soften a contraction of credit during a crisis – without necessarily taking on all the costs associated with a broad government guarantee during normal times. During normal times it would avoid the distortions in the housing market associated with a broad-based guarantee and thus reduce both moral hazard and taxpayer risk. Again, private capital would be more likely to flow to the most productive assets in the economy, private actors would be on the hook for their own risky decisions and the government would not be putting taxpayers at direct risk in backing the nation's mortgage market.

In addition to these benefits, the government would be in a better position than under Option One to manage another downturn in the housing market. As private capital pulls back, the government could better step in to ensure the availability of credit and thus help to stabilize a declining market. Though this would likely be more effective than relying only on Congress, FHA, and the Federal Reserve, there remains a significant operational challenge in designing and managing an organization that can remain small during normal economic times, yet has the capacity to take on much more business quickly during these times of need.

There are other costs to this model as well. Aside from the uncertainty around how well it would be able to scale up in times of crisis, there is the same concern with the access issues that we face with the prior option. Access to credit, particularly the pre-payable, 30-year fixed-rate mortgage, would likely be more expensive under this option than under the following one.

Option 3: Privatized system of housing finance with FHA, USDA and Department of Veterans' Affairs assistance for low- and moderate-income borrowers and catastrophic reinsurance behind significant private capital

Under this option, as in the previous options, the mortgage market outside of the FHA and other federal agency guarantee programs would be driven by private investment decisions with private capital taking the primary credit risk. However, to increase the liquidity in the mortgage market and access to mortgages for creditworthy Americans – as well as to ensure the government's ability to respond to future crises – the government would offer reinsurance for the securities of a targeted range of mortgages.

In one approach to such a system, a group of private mortgage guarantor companies that meet stringent capital and oversight requirements would provide guarantees for securities backed by mortgages that meet strict underwriting standards. A government reinsurer would then provide reinsurance to the holders of these securities, which would be paid out only if shareholders of the private mortgage guarantors have been entirely wiped out. The government reinsurer would charge a premium for this reinsurance, which would be used to cover future claims and recoup losses to protect taxpayers.

The strength of this option is that it likely provides the lowest-cost access to mortgage credit of the three options. While mortgage rates would be increased by the cost of the premium and the first-loss position of private capital, this reinsurance will likely attract a larger pool of investors to the mortgage market, increasing liquidity. This, in turn, could help to lower the prices and pricing volatility of mortgages and increase the availability of the pre-payable, 30-year fixed-rate mortgage. It will also provide a more competitive playing field for smaller lenders and community banks, which, in turn, could improve access in communities where those institutions have a good record of service. And finally, the government reinsurer's broad presence in the market could put it in a position to scale up to provide credit during a time of stress in the market more effectively.

However, this option, too, comes with costs. The increased flow of capital into the mortgage market could draw capital away from potentially more productive sectors of the economy and could artificially inflate the value of housing assets. And while the capital requirements, oversight of the private mortgage guarantors, and premiums collected to cover future losses will together help to reduce the risk to the taxpayer, the reinsurance of private-lending activity, by its nature, exposes the government to risk and moral hazard. If the oversight of the private mortgage guarantors is inadequate or the pricing of the reinsurance too low or recoupment of costs too politically difficult, then private actors in the market may take on excessive risk and the taxpayer could again bear the cost.

In choosing among these options, care must be given to designing a system that maximizes the benefits we are seeking from government involvement in the mortgage market, while minimizing the costs. We must also consider how to utilize the existing systems and assets in our housing finance system, including those at Fannie Mae and Freddie Mac, as best as possible for the benefit of the taxpayer and the American people. But design choices alone will not tell us what the best path is for the future of our mortgage system, for we are faced with difficult trade-offs. We must decide what we take to be the right balance between providing broad access to mortgages for American families, managing the risk to taxpayers, and maintaining a stable and healthy mortgage market. As we see above, these priorities are not always well aligned, so we will have to make difficult decisions as we choose the path for long-term reform.

There will of course be significant debate about how to strike this difficult balance. But we must be careful not to let that debate keep us from the immediate task at hand: we need to scale back the role of government in the mortgage market, and promote the return of private capital to a healthier, more robust mortgage market.

We will continue to seek input and consult with a wide variety of constituents, market participants, academic experts, and consumer and community organizations on our plan for reform. Given the importance of the long-term stability of the housing market and the critical role the government continues to play in the current financial circumstances, this approach to housing finance reform, built upon significant input from various stakeholders, should form the basis for a strong bi-partisan solution that results in a stronger housing finance market for all Americans.

The housing finance system *must* be reformed. It is the vital link to sustainable homeownership and rental options for millions of Americans, and it is central to our nation's economy. We allowed its flaws to go unchecked for too long, contributing to a financial collapse that has strained families, decimated communities, and pushed the economy into the worst recession since the Great Depression. The Obama Administration here provides a path of reform, which will lead to a future system with more private capital, better-aligned incentives, more oversight, and less risk to the taxpayer – in short, to a healthier, more stable system of housing finance.